Steve Sells Vans

A Division of The McGraw·Hill Companies

Columbus, Ohio

www.sra4kids.com

SRA/McGraw-Hill

A Division of The **McGraw·Hill** Companies

Printed in the United States of America.

Send all inquiries to:
SRA/McGraw-Hill
8787 Orion Place
Columbus, OH 43240-4027

ISBN 0-07-569745-9
  2 3 4 5 6 7 8 9 DBH 05 04 03 02

I am Steve.
I sell vans.

This is Pete.
Pete is a vet.
He likes the huge van.

Pete can use the huge van to
carry a giant panda.

Pete can use the huge van
to carry cute pups.
Pete the vet likes the van.

This is Val.
Val is a ranger.
She likes the tan van.

Ranger Val can use the tan
van to drive over huge rocks.

Ranger Val can use the tan
van to drive to Gem Cave.

This is Zeke.
Zeke sells ginger ale.
He likes this van.

Zeke can drive the van and sell ginger ale.
The van can make ice cubes.

Zeke drives to Gem Cave.
Zeke waves to Ranger Val.

This is Eve.
Eve likes music.
She likes this van.

Eve can put pages of music in the van.
Eve can put five children in the van.

Eve and the five children like the van.
Pete, Zeke, and Val like the music.

I am Steve.
I sell vans.
Can I sell you a van?